Days

OF

Christmas

A Collection of Seasonal Reflections

Written by M.H. Clark
Designed and illustrated by Jessica Phoenix

The Heart
of the
Season

Christmas shines with many facets. There are quiet moments, celebratory moments, moments of extraordinary happiness, festive merriment, and simple joy. There is preparation and planning, surprises to keep, and wishes to make true. And there are memories to be made that will shine and bring joy for years to come. At a time when there is so much to do and so much to celebrate, take time to savor the season and connect with all the things that make it so bright.

This book is filled with thoughts to keep you close to the heart of the season. Read one reflection each day from December 1st to Christmas Day, like an advent calendar—or choose the reflection that's right for the moment. Read one before a meal, when you wake, over tea, or at the end of a busy day. You'll find your own way to connect with these thoughts and to kindle a renewed appreciation for everything that Christmas means to you.

ANTICIPATION

Can you feel it? Good things are coming. Gifts of
true warmth and kindness, bright-shining moments
you will keep close to your heart, memories you
will savor again and again. All of this, and many
things you cannot even begin to imagine. Look
forward to all that is yet to be—with complete
delight, with simple faith. Remember that
there is still so much wonder on its way.

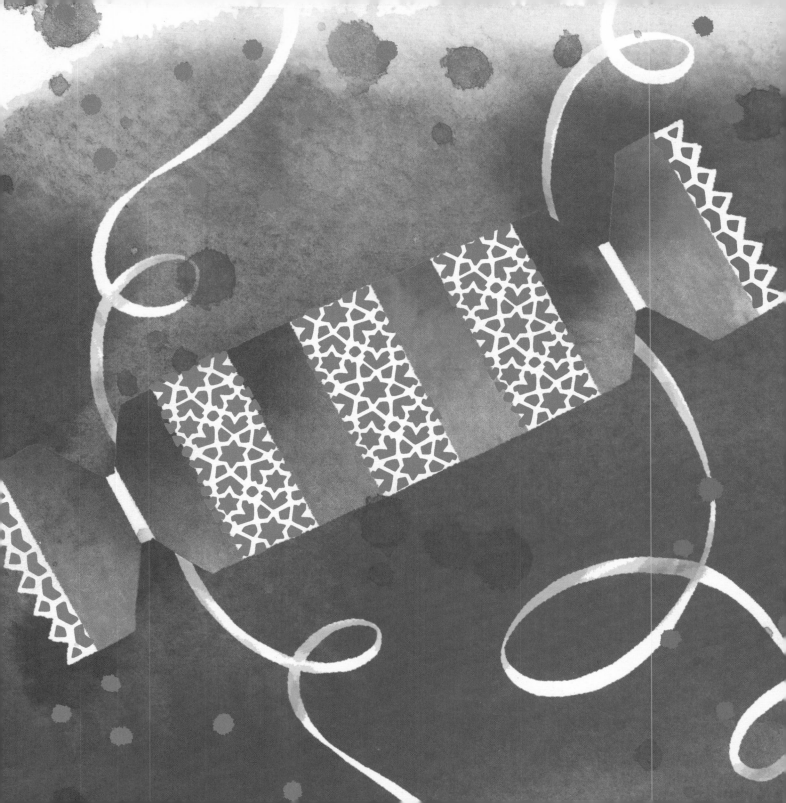

HOPE

Your heart is full of quiet desires. Some of them
are known and some of them are so new, so gentle,
you aren't even aware of them yet. But no matter
how quiet these wishes are, Christmas is a season
to nurture them, to give them a chance to grow,
to keep their flames alive. It's a season to remember
that sometimes, the unexpected is possible
in its own way and its own time.

Spirit

Spirit isn't a visible thing. It can't be

bought or wrapped or stuffed in a stocking,

but it can always be felt. And it's easy to recognize.

Because spirit speaks in the language of your heart.

And the spirit of Christmas is found in all those

things your heart responds to—timeless carols,

favorite memories, acts of generosity and kindness.

Focus on the places where spirit lives today,

and notice how your heart begins to sing.

BELIEF

At this time of year, we come heart to heart
with the things we believe—the things we know
to be true, even when we cannot find the words
or thoughts to explain. At this time of year, we
make room in our lives for miracles, for acts
of hope and faith. And the world responds.
It reminds us in hundreds of ways just how much
is possible and just how blessed we truly are.

GENEROSITY

Much has been given to us—so much that
it is easy to forget, to overlook, to let a sense of
ordinariness come between us and everything
we have. Christmas is a chance to see again,
to start anew, to simply give—and in each act
of generosity, to realize that we can afford to
give—of our time, our energy, our selves. It isn't
about the size or the cost of each gift, it's about the
chance we have been given to recognize, to notice,
to appreciate, and to pass our abundance along.

WONDER

Wonder invites astonishment. Wonder doesn't always need to understand. It reminds us that we are small beings in a big and astonishing world. Christmas is the perfect time to rekindle a sense of wonder—an appreciation for the incredible things that are all around us, a calmness in the face of great beauty. As one year draws to a close and another prepares to begin, let us welcome wonder in.

CONTENTMENT

Contentment doesn't ask a lot: a cup of hot
chocolate on a wintry afternoon, a favorite scarf,
a gingerbread man, an envelope you can't wait
to open. Contentment is at home in simplicity.
Today, search for contentment where you are.
Surprise yourself by discovering unexpected
richness in everyday things. Savor a moment in
which your heart is truly alive because it knows,
just for an instant, you have everything you need.

KINDNESS

An act of kindness is like a snowflake—there is
beauty in one and power in many. What might
seem insignificant has the potential to do so
much, because, like a sudden flurry, kindness
accumulates. Today, offer something, even if it
is small. Give something that is uniquely yours
to give. Find your own way to make your
corner of the world more beautiful.

Picture yourself lighting a candle in a quiet church
or standing in the cold night air and staring at the
stars. Picture a snow that has swept everything
clean and bright and new. Picture yourself in a
moment of perfect calm. A moment of silence.
In this moment, nothing is asked of you but to
be exactly who and what you are. Find stillness
today wherever you are, and carry it
forward from this moment on.

REMEMBRANCE

The years change us—they change our
holidays, and they change the way we celebrate.
Some years bring us joyful additions, and some
bring us times of parting. At Christmas, we reflect
and we remember. We unfold old memories,
we treasure them, we think back, and we offer
our gratitude for the people whose hearts and
hands have made our lives all that they are.
In remembrance, thoughts, and in prayer,
these loved ones are always near.

TRADITION

These are the things you know, and the things you love. The ornaments you unwrap, and the rush of memories that come along with them. The recipes you know by heart, with flavors that the years do not change. These are the songs you sing, the gifts you give, all those places where the season comes to life. Cherish the way that time has made these things all that they are. Honor the lives these traditions have touched. Create new rituals. And keep the memories strong.

WARMTH

In a season of darkness, warmth changes everything. Warmth makes a home in the night, saves a place at the table, turns a moment into a memory. There is the quiet warmth of a candle in a window, the blazing warmth of a fireplace, the slow-burning warmth of a person who makes your life more complete. Today, seek out ways to be a mirror for the warmth that you receive from others; reflect it back to the waiting world.

TOGETHERNESS

We send Christmas cards down the street
and around the world, with well-wishes in
each envelope. We wrap presents with joyful
expectation, we make phone calls and send emails,
and find small and big ways to say hello, to share
a smile, to spread holiday cheer. We seek out time
to be together, because we recognize that the people
we love are the best reasons to celebrate.

Family

Our families are the people we build our lives around—the people who know us in and out and love us just the same. They're the ones who remind us that wherever we are, however old we are, we need people who feel like home. Today, take a moment to reflect on the old memories and look forward to building new ones. Send a word of appreciation, share a favorite photograph, and find new ways to show your love.

EXCITEMENT

Have you found it yet? There's something incredible in this day. In a season when everything is sparkling and shining, allow yourself to get carried away. Allow yourself to look forward to something. Give yourself a chance to appreciate the sweetness that's all around you. Let excitement give you momentum, and let it remind you that no matter how much there is to be done, there are plenty of good surprises in store.

Once the presents are opened and the plates
are cleared and the fire has burned down to
embers, there is still something left of Christmas.
It's warm and it's steady. And it lasts. That thing
is love. It is in and around all of us at this time
of year—it is the reason for our being together,
and the true heart of the holiday. Today, find love
and keep love at the center of all that you do.

ENTHUSIASM

It starts like a quiet fire in your heart, but then
it builds. Bit by bit, things seem warmer. Suddenly,
everything is glittering, everything is brilliant,
and lit up with joy. Share your enthusiasm, pass
along your radiance, bring spirit to even the little
things you do. Watch as the world around you
responds, as the excitement you send out
brightens everything it touches.

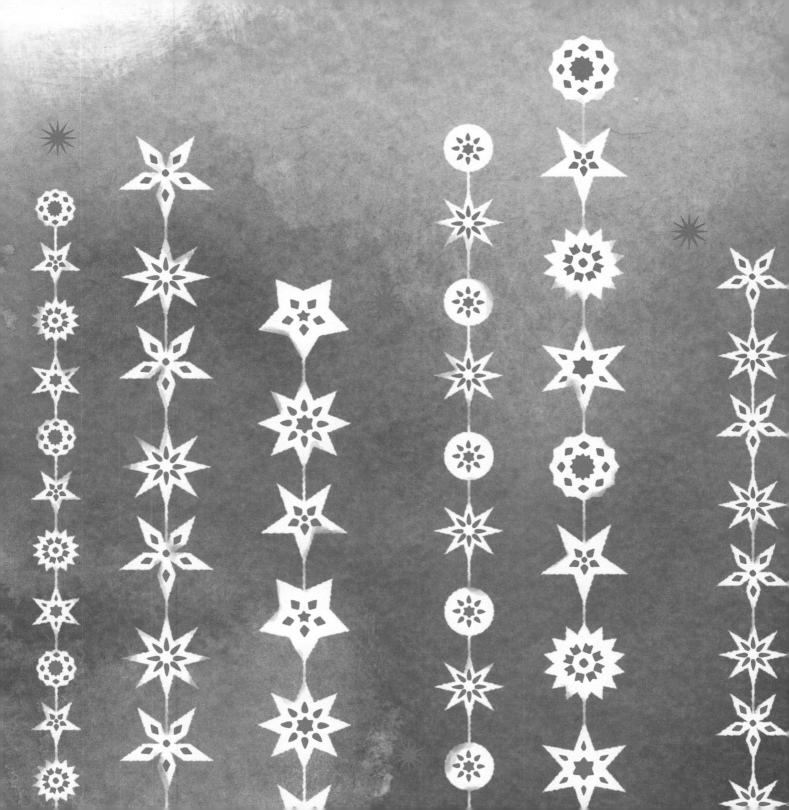

FESTIVITY

There's festivity in every single twinkling
light, every ringing bell, and every sugar cookie.
It's in each wreath and garland and candy cane.
These bright things create a spirit of joy and
celebration—a joyful occasion that unites us all
in warmth and good spirits. And all you have
to do to take part is open your eyes,
open your heart, and join in.

MAGIC

There was a time when you believed.
You trusted in the unknown. You understood
that the world was larger than you and filled
with astonishing possibility. You looked,
every day, for marvelous things. And because
you looked, you found them. Why not begin again
to find amazement everywhere? To welcome
the unexpected? Look around you today,
and see what magic can be found.

Surprise

What makes a surprise so special? The fact that you weren't expecting it. A surprise is the perfect reminder that there's something extraordinary in every day, just waiting to find you, to delight you, maybe to even sweep you off your feet. Start noticing surprises—even the little ones: a favorite song, an unexpected call, the gift of an extra hour. You'll discover wonderful things where you least thought they'd be, and that's where true merriment lives.

DELIGHT

Delight radiates from the inside out.
It puts sparkle in your eyes because there's
gladness in your soul. Delight changes whatever
it touches, and makes everything richer. Today,
take delight in the work you do for others, in
simple moments of satisfaction, and in all that this
season holds. And when you are given something
unexpected, let a wave of delight catch you,
hold you, and make you shine.

GRATITUDE

It is always a season for gratitude, always the
right moment to tell people that we appreciate
the things that they do, and all that they are.
But Christmas is a time when our gratitude is
even more present and more profound. As we look
back on the year that has been, we are filled with
appreciation—not just for the delights that come
wrapped, but for the things we receive every day.
This is a time to cherish both the giver and the gift.

JOY

Joy ties a bright bow on everything. Joy sees the sparkle in the snowflake, the potential in the day. And joy finds a reason to sing. Living this day in joy doesn't mean there will be less stress or fewer things to do. It simply means you will see the gold thread that runs through it all. It means you will be able to find sweetness and levity wherever you are. Let joy carry you, let it uplift you, let it light your way.

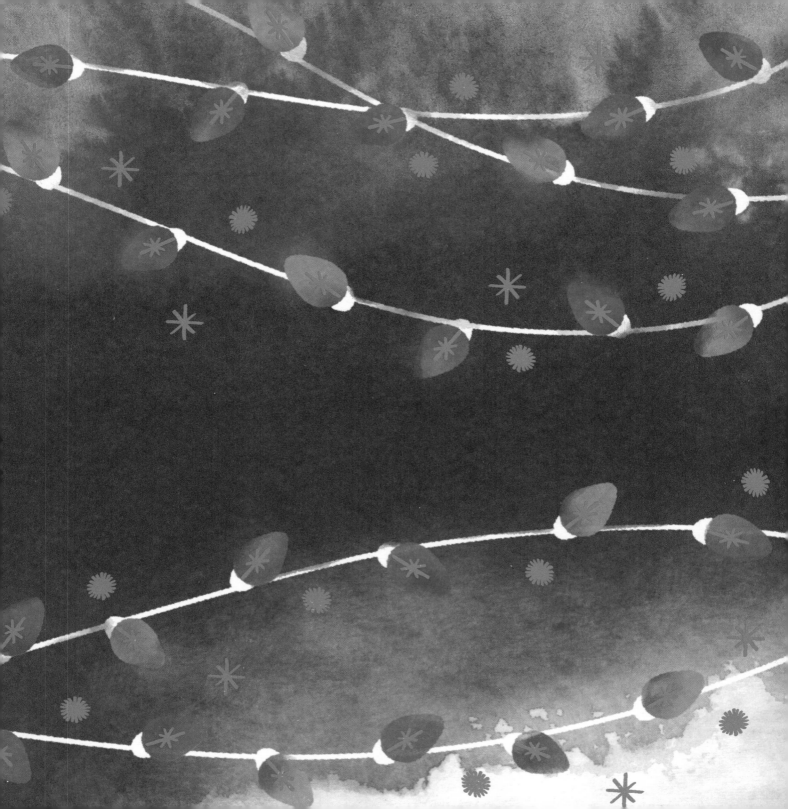

CONNECTION

Take this moment to think about all the lives you have touched and all the lives that have touched yours in return. Think of the gifts you have given, the gifts you have received—even gifts as simple as a phone call, a smile, a shared moment. Envision that each act of giving ties us together, connects us with a spark and a light. Remember that we are all touched by that light, bound together by it, connected by kindness and by love.

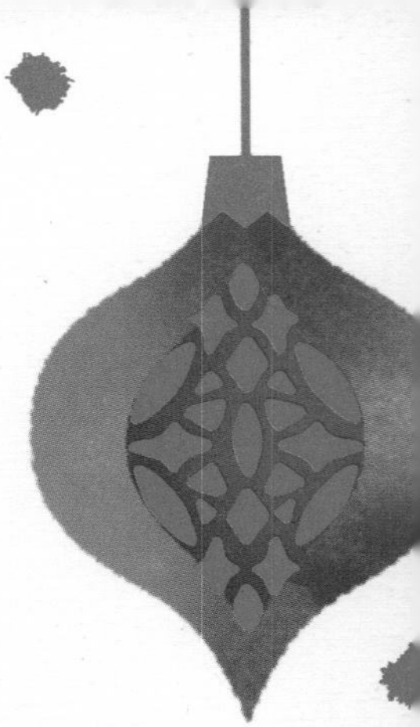

CELEBRATION

There are lots of ways to have a celebration—it can be over the top with baubles and shine, or quieter and more subdued. It can be loud with music and laughter and clinking glasses, or simple and serene. But there's really only one thing you need in order to have a celebration: something to celebrate. And since there's something worth celebrating in every single day, why not start now? Why not turn this moment into something to remember?

The Coming Year

In the little nest of days between
Christmas and the New Year, take time—time
to hope, to wish, to plan. Time to imagine what
your year will hold, and to decide how you will
make room for all the things that matter. Celebrate
the year that has been with reverence; welcome the
year that will soon unfold with anticipation and joy.
And remember that dark winter nights are made
for dreaming of all the good things yet to be.

COMPENDIUM®

live inspired.

With special thanks to the entire Compendium family.

CREDITS:
Written by: M.H. Clark
Designed by: Jessica Phoenix
Edited by: Amelia Riedler
Creative Direction by: Julie Flahiff

Library of Congress Control Number: 2014930142
ISBN: 978-1-938298-29-5

1st printing. Printed in China with soy and metallic inks.